C for Cristero

ISBN 979-8-8691-7794-0

Printed in the United States of America
IngramSpark
14 Ingram Blvd.
La Vergne, TN 37086

Introduction

The Cristero War is very significant in Mexican history.

It involved not just a civil war that broke out over church and state issues in Mexico but also attracted the attention of international figures such as the United States and the Vatican. Due to the Cristeros War, Mexico became a near totalitarian dictatorship that is still relevant because it also influenced Mexico in the present day.

Background

Let's start with the background of the Cristeros

War.

The Cristeros War originated with a conflict

between church and state in Mexico in the

1920s.

More specifically, there was peaceful resistance

by Mexican Catholics against the enforcement

of the anticlerical provisions of the constitution

that targeted Mexican Catholics.

However, conflict broke out in 1926, and

violent uprisings began in 1927.

The war was between two factions: the

Cristeros and the Mexican government.

The Cristeros were rebels who invoked the

name of Jesus Christ under the title "Cristo

Rey" or "Christ the King" in English.

The Cristeros were also made up of the

Feminine Brigades of St. Joan of Arc, which

was a brigade of women who assisted the rebels

in smuggling guns and ammunition.

The rebellion attracted the attention of Pope

Pius XI, who issued a series of papal

encyclicals between 1925 and 1937.

On December 11, 1925, the pontiff issued Quas

primas, establishing the Feast of Christ the

King, to honor the Cristeros defense of

Christianity.

On November 18, 1926, Pope Pius XI issued

Iniquis afflictisque, which condemned the

violent anti-clerical persecution in Mexico.

Despite the Mexican government's promises to end its persecution, it continued the persecution of the Church.

In response, Pius issued Acerba animi on September 29, 1932, which also condemned the persecution of Catholics in Mexico.

As one can see, the Cristero War was very significant, not just for Mexico but for the Catholic Church as well.

Key Issues

The biggest problem regarding church and state involved the Mexican Constitution of 1917. Also known as the Political Constitution of the United Mexican States, it was drafted by the Constitutional Congress summoned by Venustiano Carranza, the President of Mexico at the time, in September 1916 and was approved on February 5, 1917.

Three of its 136 articles, more specifically Article 3, Article 27, and Article 130, contained very secular sections, restricting the power and influence of the Roman Catholic Church.

One example in Article 3 states that

"educational services shall be secular and,

therefore, free of any religious orientation.".

These articles also provided for mandatory state

registration of all churches and religious

congregations and placed a series of restrictions

on priests and ministers of all religions, which

included being banned from holding public

office, blocking their ability to work on behalf

of political parties or candidates, and not

allowing them to inherit from persons other than close blood relatives.

These articles also allowed the state to regulate the number of priests in each region by reducing the number to zero, prohibiting the wearing of religious garb, and rejecting offenders from a trial by jury.

Due to three articles in the Mexican Constitution, Catholics were persecuted, which eventually led to civil war.

Key Events

Various events also led to a rebellion by Catholics.

Violence occurred throughout the 1920s by Catholics against the Mexican government.

In 1926, following the passage of strict anticlerical criminal laws and enforcement, in addition to peasant revolts against land reform in the heavily Catholic regions of north-central Mexico and a crackdown on popular religious celebrations such as mass and fiestas.

Not only that, but guerrilla operations transformed into a serious armed revolt against the government, which caused Catholic and

anticlerical groups to turn to terrorism as a

means of warfare.

Of all the uprisings against the Mexican

government in the 1920s, the Cristero War was

the most devastating and had the most long-

term effects.

Although many Cristeros continued fighting,

they no longer did so with the support of the

church.

Persecution of Catholics and anti-government

terrorist attacks continued into the 1940s, when

the remaining organized Cristero groups were

incorporated into the Sinarquista Party.

Therefore, riots, uprisings, and terrorism led to

rebellion between the Cristeros and the

Mexican Government.

Diplomacy

Diplomacy was also used during the Cristeros War.

In 1927, US ambassador to Mexico, Dwight Whitney Morrow, initiated a series of breakfast meetings with Mexican President Calles where they would discuss a range of issues, such as religious uprisings, oil, and immigration. Morrow wanted the conflict to end both for regional security and to help find a solution to the oil problem in the United States.

Also, Fr. John J. Burke of the National Catholic

Welfare Conference aided Morrow in his

efforts.

However, former Mexican President Alvaro

Obregon had been elected after Calles' term

ended.

While Obregon had been more merciful to

Catholics during his time in office, it was also

generally accepted by the Cristeros that Calles

was Obregon's "puppet leader."

Unfortunately, diplomacy failed to work, and

violence escalated between the Cristeros and

the Mexican government.

Smuggling

Smuggling was also a common practice during the Cristeros War.

Guns, ammunition, bootlegged liquor, illegal drugs, and counterfeit cash were among the most common objects that smugglers have carried across the US-Mexico border in recent years.

However, during the 1920s and 1930s, Mexican and American citizens began smuggling religious paraphernalia, such as scapulars, rosaries, images, and printed materials that were created in the United States by Catholics from both countries and planned for distribution within Mexico.

Among the people who trafficked this religious material were young Mexican migrants, priests and nuns, members of the Knights of Columbus, and many other otherwise law-abiding citizens.

At the same time, large numbers of Mexican citizens began sneaking across the border to attend Catholic Mass.

The Cristero War was definitely significant, as

it was the first time smuggling occurred along

the U.S.-Mexico border.

Immigration

Immigration was another huge issue that began during the Cristero War.

The US-Mexico border was so heavily affected by the religious conflict that many Mexican states along the border began sending migrants to the United States to escape the war-torn country.

As a result, thousands of immigrants were arriving in Texas, southern California, and other border states to find work and a new home.

After the outbreak of the Cristero War, the

Mexican government began deporting Catholic

clergy and political exiles, which caused over

2,500 priests, nuns, and members of religious

orders to arrive in the United States during the

late 1920s.

These religious immigrants settled in urban

areas where there were large and growing

Mexican communities, such as Los Angeles, El

Paso, and San Antonio.

The conditions of migration during the late 1920s also helped create a movement of Cristero supporters in the United States. This movement spanned the borderlands and eventually even extended into the growing Mexican communities of the Midwest. During the 1920s and 1930s, these Catholic supporters organized clubs and associations, sponsored religious processions and other public activities within their neighborhoods, and lobbied politicians on both sides of the border in support of the Cristeros' cause.

Many of these supporters also participated in secret underground efforts to help the Cristeros from abroad, including raising money, recruiting soldiers from among the young migrant population, and printing leaflets and religious texts to be sent back to Mexico. A few of them even organized armed religious revolts along the border, and others contributed money for guns and ammunition that could be sent to the Cristero troops on the battlefields in the Mexican heartland.

Immigration was a huge deal during the

Cristero War, as it helped increase their power

and support and was a precursor to the

immigration that continues to occur along the

U.S.-Mexico border.

Knights of Columbus

The Knights of Columbus also contributed to the Cristeros' war effort.

The famous Catholic fraternal organization launched a fundraising campaign known as the Million Dollar Fund, which produced pamphlets in English and Spanish denouncing the anticlerical Mexican government and publicizing the effect of the Cristero War on Mexico's Catholics.

This printed material, along with the literature produced by Mexicans in the United States, was passed so frequently into Mexico during the war years that the Mexican government issued

specific warnings about the problem, including

a directive for border guards to be on the

lookout for nuns and other Catholic women,

who were known to bring Catholic propaganda

into the country underneath their dresses.

The Knights of Columbus were a valuable ally

of the Cristeros as they helped bring

Catholicism back into Mexico.

Mexican Government

It should also be noted that the Mexican government was a very powerful foe that the Cristeros faced.

Mexican President Calles saw the Catholic Church as a relic that needed to be purged. This caused Mexican bishops to debate and consult with the Holy See and eventually suspend public worship on July 31, 1926. Three bishops went into hiding, while the remaining bishops left the country in exile.

On August 1, 1926, for the first time in more than four hundred years, priests in Mexico offered Mass.

It should be noted, however, that priests who remained in Mexico faced two choices: cooperation with the government or a life on the run.

Those who cooperated were forced to abandon their parishes, move to urban areas, and register with their state governments, which now had the power to set clerical quotas.

In the state of Tobasco, for example, Governor

Tomas Canabal restricted the number of priests

in his state to six, one for every thirty thousand

citizens.

Governor Canabal also demanded that the

priests in his state take wives and named his

children Lenin, Lucifer, and Satan after he

identified himself as "The Personal Enemy of

God.".

However, a few courageous priests refused to

register and went into hiding by roaming

Mexico by night and in disguise in order to

bring the sacraments to the faithful.

If these priests were caught, they were arrested,

fined, jailed, tortured, or executed.

Following the suspension of public worship by

the Mexican government, the National League

for the Defense of Religious Liberty circulated

a petition signed by two million Mexicans who

demanded constitutional reform.

Unfortunately, the Mexican government denied

the existence of the petition, which caused

Mexican citizens to boycott government

transportation, energy, and entertainment.

Sadly, the boycott failed because Mexico's

wealthy complained to the government, which

caused federal police to break up picket lines.

By January of 1927, many Mexican Catholics

concluded that peaceful protests would not

work, and they took up arms against the

government.

As one can see, the Mexican government was a

powerful entity that was capable of squashing

any peaceful protest or opposition.

Women

Women also played a very large role during the Cristero War.

More specifically, Cristero support was very strong thanks to an extensive logistics network run by the Feminine Brigades of St. Joan of Arc, a Catholic women's organization affiliated with the Union Popular.

The women devised creative and underground ways to keep soldiers supplied, such as special vests for smuggling ammunition out of federal factories and secret workshops for the production of homemade explosives, such as

grenades made out of jelly tins.

These courageous twenty-five thousand ladies

also carried messages written on silk and

hidden within the soles of shoes between units.

All of their activities were carried out under an

oath of secrecy that was never broken.

If it weren't for these strong-willed women, the

Cristeros would not have the advantage of

espionage and smuggling against the Mexican

government.

The Cristero Effect

As a result of the Cristeros actions, President Calles felt threatened, and the Mexican government was weakening.

The Cristero war was costing the Mexican government 96 million pesos a year, which was more than a third of its annual budget.

Calles' scorched-earth policy against the Cristeros also harmed the Mexican economy.

Calles' policy of relocating 30 percent of the rural population of Mexico to urban areas in order to eliminate Cristero support created increasing anger against the Mexican

government.

As a result, half a million Mexicans left the

country, and 60 percent of the Mexican military

were killed.

Despite the Mexican government's power and

authority, it caused many problems due to poor

leadership by President Calles.

The Ku Klux Klan

The Ku Klux Klan was another American group

that was involved in the Cristeros war.

For example, high-ranking members of the

KKK offered President Calles $10,000 to help

fight the Catholic Church.

The offer was a result of the Knights of

Columbus secretly offering the Cristeros $1,000

for guns and ammunition.

The offer was made after Calles sent a private

telegram to the Mexican Ambassador to France,

stating that the Catholic Church in Mexico is a

political movement and must be eliminated in

order to proceed with a socialist government free of religious hypnotism, which fools the people. Within one year without the sacraments, the people will forget the faith.

As one can see, the KKK was a valuable ally to the Mexican government in terms of financial aid, which paralleled the Knights of Columbus' allegiance to the Cristeros.

Problems

Despite the many successes of the Cristeros,

many problems arose for them.

For example, many churches, schools, and

rectories were in government hands.

Also, Cristeros that were not willing to move

out of their states were taken prisoner and

executed.

There were also mass executions, and reports of

Cristero veterans being hunted down and killed

lasted until the 1950s, and thousands of them

lost their lives after the war had been declared

over.

Most state governments closed churches, which caused priests to vanish or go on the run again.

Also, schoolteachers were required to take a public oath of atheism and to promise to teach against the Catholic religion.

Not only that, but Archbishop Diaz, a powerful figure of the Catholic Church in Mexico, was thrown in jail and forced to help the Mexican government, which was seen as an act of betrayal to the Cristeros.

Cristeros were also tortured in order to force them to reveal their military secrets and to deny the Catholic faith.

Electric shock, burning with blowtorches, hanging by thumbs, and breaking bones were common practices of torture.

It was also common to drag prisoners behind a horse and then quarter them alive, flay the soles of their feet, and then force them to walk on rock salt.

The most infamous action against the Cristeros was crucifying them on telephone poles.

It should also be noted that priests captured by

the Mexican government were hanged or shot.

Miguel Pro

The most famous of the martyred priests is

Miguel Pro, unjustly implicated in a failed

assassination attempt on Calles' successor,

Alvaro Obregon.

Pro died before a firing squad with his arms

outstretched like our Lord crucified, shouting

"¡Viva Cristo Rey!"

Calles ordered that Miguel Pro's execution be

photographed, in hopes that the grisly images

would discourage Catholics from supporting the

Cristeros.

However, the photos encouraged support for the Cristeros all over the world, which led Calles to forbid papers to print them.

Although Miguel Pro was not part of any armed rebellion, his martyrdom inspired others to take up arms in support of the Cristeros.

Despite all the persecution, betrayal, violence, torture, death, and martyrdom, many Cristero died bravely, and their deaths inspired other Mexicans to take up arms against the Mexican government.

Battles

In 1926, many rebellions and battles occurred across Mexico between Catholics and the Mexican government.

In Guadalajara, Jalisco, some 400 armed Catholics shut themselves in the Church of Our Lady of Guadalupe.

They exchanged gunfire with federal troops and surrendered when they ran out of ammunition.

According to US consular sources, the battle resulted in 18 dead and 40 wounded.

The following day, in Sahuayo, Michoacan, 240 government soldiers stormed the parish church.

The priest and his vicar were killed in the ensuing violence.

Government agents also staged a purge of the Chalchihuites, Zacatecas, chapter of the Association of Catholic Youth and executed its spiritual adviser, Father Luis Batiz Sainz.

The execution caused a band of ranchers, led by Pedro Quintanar, to seize the local treasury and to declare themselves in rebellion.

At the height of the rebellion, they held a region including the entire northern part of Jalisco.

Luis Navarro Origel, the mayor of Penjamo, Guanajuato, led another uprising as well. His men were defeated by federal troops in the open land around the town but retreated into the mountains, where they continued guerrilla warfare.

In support of the two guerrilla Apache clans, the Chavez and Trujillos helped smuggle arms, ammunition, and supplies from the US state of New Mexico.

This was followed by an uprising in Durango, led by Trinidad Mora, and another rebellion in southern Guanajuato, led by former General

Rodolfo Gallegos.

Both rebel leaders adopted guerrilla tactics

since their forces were no match for the federal

troops.

Meanwhile, rebels in Jalisco, particularly in the

region northeast of Guadalajara, quietly began

assembling forces.

Led by 27-year-old Rene Capistran Garza, the

leader of the Mexican Association of Catholic

Youth, the region would become the main focal

point of the rebellion.

The formal rebellion began on January 1, 1927,

with a manifesto sent by Garza, "A la Nacion,"

or "To the Nation.".

It declared that the hour of battle has sounded

and that the hour of victory belongs to God.

With the declaration, the state of Jalisco, which

had been seemingly quiet since the Guadalajara

church uprising, exploded with conflict.

Bands of rebels moving in the "Los Altos"

region northeast of Guadalajara began seizing

villages and were often armed with only ancient

muskets and clubs.

The Cristeros' battle cry was ¡Viva Cristo Rey!

¡Viva la Virgen de Guadalupe! (Long live

Christ the King! (Long live the Virgin of

Guadalupe!).

The rebels had scarce logistical supplies and

relied heavily on the Feminine Brigades of St.

Joan of Arc and raids on towns, trains, and

ranches to supply themselves with money,

horses, ammunition, and food.

By contrast, the Calles government was

supplied with arms and ammunition by the US

government later in the war.

In at least one battle, US pilots provided air

support for the federal army against the Cristero

rebels.

The Calles government failed at first to take the

threat seriously.

The rebels did well against the agraristas, a

rural militia recruited throughout Mexico, and

the Social Defense forces, the local militia, but

were at first always defeated by regular federal

troops, who guarded the main cities.

The federal army then had 79,759 men.

When the Jalisco federal commander, General

Jesus Ferreira, moved in on the rebels, he

matter-of-factly wired to army headquarters that

it would be less of a campaign than a hunt.

The rebels planned their battles fairly well,

despite the fact that most of them had little to

no previous military experience.

The most successful rebel leaders were Jesus

Degollado Guizar, a pharmacist; Victoriano

Ramirez, a ranch hand; and two priests, Jose

Aristeo Pedroza and Jose Reyes Vega.

Jesus Degollado Guizar

Jesus Degollado Guizar was a pharmacist turned general in the Cristero War.

His parents were very religious and instilled ideologies in accordance with the Catholic religion.

In the 1920s, Guizar lived in Atotonilco el Alto, in Jalisco, which is where he joined the Catholic Association of Mexican Youth (ACJM) and another organization named Union of Mexican Catholics, joining Don Esteban de la Parra and Mr. Jose Mendoza.

These associations would be known

underground as the U.

In 1926, in the face of conflicts that arose

during the presidency of Plutarco Elias Calles,

Guizar decided to join the Christian Liberating

Army.

In mid-1927, the National League for Religious

Defense decided to appoint him as Major

General and Chief Operating Officer in the

Western Region, which included West

Michoacan, southern Jalisco, and Nayarit.

General Guizar was responsible for carrying out

the Conventions with the Government, which was the one that laid the foundations for the discharge of the Cristero Army as a National Guard for the month of July 1929, since Monsignor Leopoldo Ruiz y Flores, who was Archbishop of Morelia, and Emilio Portes Gil, who was then the president of Mexico, signed the peace agreement on July 21, 1929.

In the end, the agreements signed were decreed by some points that were not respected, such as stopping persecuting the generals, chiefs, officers, and Christian soldiers.

The murder of Christian soldiers continued silently, killing a greater number of officers than in the three years of the Cristero War. In order not to be killed, Guizar decided to live the rest of his life in hiding until 1957, when he died of old age.

Guizar was responsible for drafting the peace treaty that ended the Cristero war due to his negotiation skills and experience as a peacemaker.

Enrique Gorostieta

Enrique Gorostieta was a major figure in the Cristeros War.

Born in Monterrey into a prominent Mexican-Basque family, Enrique Gorostieta had a typically secular education.

His father, an attorney and businessman, had personalties with Victoriano Huerta, and Enrique was encouraged by his mother to take up a military career. He enrolled at the Heroic Military College of Chapultepec in 1906.

Upon graduation in May 1911, the same month Porfirio Diaz stepped down from the

Presidency, Gorostieta, as an advisor to

Victoriano Huerta, served on campaigns against

Emiliano Zapata in September 1911 and against

Pascual Orozco in April–May 1912.

During Huerta's short dictatorship from 1913 to

1914, Gorostieta's father was Secretary of the

Treasury.

During the Mexican Revolution, he served in

the Federal Army of Counterrevolutionary

Forces under dictator Victoriano Huerta.

After Huerta's fall, Goristieta fought with Juan

Andreu Almazan but soon fled Mexico for

Cuba and later the United States.

Upon his return to Mexico, he worked as a soap

manufacturer but found the work boring and

sought a return to military activity.

In 1927, the National League for the Defense of

Religious Liberty chose him to lead the

Cristeros, an army of Catholic rebels fighting

against the government forces of President

Plutarco Elias Calles.

Although Gorostieta was originally a liberal
and a skeptic, he eventually wore a cross
around his neck and spoke openly of his
reliance on God.

Gorostieta's motivation for taking command of
the rebels was not only the high salary he was
offered (about 3000 pesos per month, or twice
the salary of a regular Army general), but also
his political ambition.

Gorostieta's 1928 "Plan de Los Altos" called
for changes to the 1917 Constitution's Article
27 (which the Cristeros saw as restricting the

rights of Catholics) and installing a Gorostieta regime in the country.

Gorostieta believed in a return to the Juarez-inspired 1857 Constitution's view of non-interference and toleration for religion rather than the Calles' administration's reading of the 1917 Constitution as demanding subordination of religious organizations to the state.

Although openly contemptuous of his subordinates' religious faith (several of his officers were priests), he respected the military acumen of the Jalisco farmers under his command and believed he could turn them into

a professional fighting force equal to the regular

army.

Gorstieta's importance as a Cristero leader was

in bringing military discipline to an

unorganized insurgency.

He is credited with turning Cristero "armies"

into a single Cristero Army, which was winning

battles in the limited region where it operated in

rural Jalisco, Michoacan, Colima, and

Zacatecas.

However, without support from the Mexican church or the Vatican and torn by internal dissension, the Cristeros were largely irrelevant as a political or military force as a negotiated settlement was worked out between the Vatican and the Mexican state over interpretations of the Church's rights under the Constitution. Nineteen days before a cessation of hostilities, based on an agreement worked out by U.S. Ambassador Dwight Morrow between Pope Pius XI and Mexican bishop Pascual Diaz y Barreto, was to take effect, Gorostieta was killed following a Mexican government intelligence operation on June 2, 1929.

With the movement rapidly collapsing, Gorostieta was attempting a retreat into Michoacan, where he hoped to recruit followers and continue the rebellion.

A federal officer, who had infiltrated Gorostieta's inner circle, tipped off the Mexican cavalry to the general's presence in Atotonilco, Jalisco, and killed him in a short firefight.

Gorostieta's military leadership essentially made him the commander-in-chief of the Cristeros.

Victoriano Ramirez

Victoriano Ramirez was another major figure in the Cristero War.

Ramirez, like many children living in the rural areas of Los Altos during the late 19th century, never attended school.

The was never taught to read or write, but his parents taught him how to pray and taught him basic life skills.

Ramirez 's father, a farmer, barely made enough money with which to sustain the family, and his mother tended to the household, caring for him and his siblings while educating them on matters such as behavior as well as the Catholic religion.

During his teenage years, Ramirez was taught how to protect livestock and how to farm. Legend holds that once, when the escaped from a prison in San Miguel el Alto, Jalisco, where the was waiting for a murder trial after a quarrel, a detachment of fourteen armed men went to look for him on a hill.

Forced to fight against his pursuers, Ramirez hid among the crags of a ravine, and after a long firefight, the killed all his opponents.

When the was sure of his victory, the took the

field and picked up the fourteen arms of his

victims and sent them to the mayor of San

Miguel with a message, advising him "not to

send such few people," earning him the name

"El Catorce" (The Fourteen).

Ramirez was among the first to join the Cristero

rebellion.

The was one of the few Cristeros who did not

desert the fight in May of 1927.

The commanded the "Fourteen Dragons"

squadron, which was part of the San Julian

regiment under the command of General
Miguel Hernandez.

His first acts as a Cristero were spoken of as
legendary feats, and tradition goes that when
"Callistas" (federal troops) heard the cry of
"Viva El Catorce!" it struck fear in their hearts
during fighting.

Additionally, Ramirez also had a reputation for
superb accuracy as a marksman.

On March 15, 1927, the Battle of San Julian
began, and "El Catorce" had to resist a day of
federal charges by General Espiridion

Rodriguez before General Miguel Hernandez arrived the next day to support him. Eventually, the battle resulted in a Cristero victory, and the federal army suffered its worst defeat in the entire war.

The difficulties that arose between Ramirez and his companions began with organizational reforms that General Enrique Gorostieta Velarde deemed necessary to establish between contingent Cristeros.

Ramirez felt that his authority was being undermined, which put a number of obstacles in the way of the proposed new organization. In view of his attitude, the was relieved of his duties and banned from having armed men, except for a small escort.

Ramirez did not obey these orders, and as the was liked by the people of San Miguel el Alto, they increased his armed escorts.

Father Aristeo Pedroza invited him to refocus on the Cristero struggle, but Victoriano refused.

These refusals antagonized other Cristero

leaders, and Aristeo Pedroza,

Heriberto Navarrete and Mario Valdes

eventually pursued Ramirez with 300 men.

By then, Ramirez was fortified at the top of El

Carretero, along with 100 colleagues.

Ramirez was eventually arrested and accused of

embezzlement, insubordination, and resistance

to higher orders.

For these accusations, Father Aristeo Pedroza

ordered his execution, and to avoid commotions

amongst the Cristeros, as El Catorce was highly

esteemed, it was resolved immediately to fulfill the sentence.

The details surrounding Ramirez's death are uncertain and based on various accounts.

One account states that, in order to avoid the popular uproar of the locals in Tepatitlan, Valdes had Ramirez stabbed to death in a discrete manner.

Another account states that at the time of his execution, the barricaded himself in his cell, so they had to break down the door with a battering ram to lead him to the place of execution.

However, the jumped out with the intention of snatching the rifle of the nearest man, but was mortally wounded by a bullet to the chest.

The most commonly known account states that the died during a failed ambush of Mexican soldiers after being killed by machine gun fire after the successfully stole a cannon from the Mexican government.

Victoriano Ramirez was a legendary one-man army that was like a real-life Rambo who took on impossible odds and did what was necessary

to bring back Catholicism to Mexico.

Jose Aristeo Pedroza

Jose Aristeo Pedroza was a Catholic priest turned Cristero Brigade General.

In 1911, he entered the seminary of Guzman City.

In 1923, he was ordained a priest.

Due to pressure from the federal government, Pedroza joins the National League for the Defense of Religious Freedoms.

Rising up in arms in early 1927, he and fellow priest Jose Reyes Vega commanded over 700 men.

On October 30, 1927, together with General

Carlos Blanco and fully authorized by General

Enrique Gorostieta, he organized the Ayo

Regiment, in which he would be in charge with

the rank of Colonel, participating in various

battles, the most important being the Battle of

Arandas of 1927, where the Mexican

Government suffered 100 casualties.

Due to his efficiency as a military leader in

battles and skirmishes, he was promoted to

Brigadier General under the command of "the

Brigade of the Highs."

In March 1928, along with General Gorostieta, he attacked and took the Plaza de San Juan de los Lagos by defeating the Mesican Government forces with greater and better arsenals.

He would eventually lose the Battle of Cerro Gordo, where he lost his second in command, Abraham Duenas.

On March 16, 1929, Father Pedroza ordered the execution of General Victoriano "El Catorce" Ramirez, who decided to serve his sentence in a questionable trial.

Pedroza mobilized his forces in an attempt to take the Mexican capital, even though it was not carried out because of the impossibility of taking a train from Poncitlan to Guadalajara.

The last event of the Cristero War in San Francisco del Rincon was an attack carried out by Father Pedroza and Lauro Rocha on April 5, 1929, firing up fierce combat in the vicinity of what is now the Cuauhtemoc Colony.

Upon the death of General Gorostieta in June 1929, Pedroza renamed "The Brigade of the

Highlands" to "The Enrique Gorostieta

Brigade" and then entered the city of Tepatitlan.

During the arrangements that were made on

July 21, 1929, Pedroza presented himself to the

Chief of Military Operations of Jalisco,

amnestied, and withdrew to Arandas.

Despite the amnesty on July 3, 1929, Pedroza

was captured.

Pedroza died after 25 of his ribs were fractured,

his jaw was broken, and he was shot to death on

July 4, 1929.

After his death, the Cristero chiefs of the state of Guanajuato were killed, including Luciano Serrano, Primitivo Jimenez, and Jose Padron.

In Zacatecas, almost all the Cristero officers, such as Pedro Quintanar and Porfirio Mallorquin, were killed as well.

Pedroza was a martyred priest who was responsible for an amnesty deal to be reached between the Cristeros and the Mexican Government.

Jose Reyes Vega

Jose Reyes Vega was a Mexican priest who participated in the Cristero War as a general.

He was one of the most popular generals during the war and was known as "Father Vega.".

An atypical priest, Vega was known as a drinker and womanizer, as well as for his murderous behavior.

After one engagement, he had federal prisoners stabbed to death to save ammunition.

On February 23, 1927, the Cristeros defeated federal troops for the first time at San Francisco del Rincon, Guanajuato, followed by another victory at San Julian, Jalisco.

However, they quickly began to lose in the face of superior federal forces, retreated into remote areas, and constantly fled federal soldiers.

Most of the leadership of the revolt in the state of Jalisco was forced to flee to the US, although Ramirez and Vega remained.

In April 1927, the leader of the civilian wing of the Cristiada, Anacleto Gonzalez Flores, was captured, tortured, and killed.

The media and the government declared victory, and plans were made for a re-education campaign in the areas that had rebelled.

On April 19, 1927, an event took place that almost succeeded in extinguishing the revolution.

Vega led a raid against a train in La Barca, Jalisco, said to be carrying a shipment of money and gold to the Bank of Mexico.

In a shootout that followed with the army escort, Vega's younger brother was killed.

Maddened with grief, he had the wooden cars

doused with gasoline, and 51 civilian

passengers were burned alive.

The atrocity helped to turn public opinion

against the Cristeros.

Vega was also known for mounting an attack

on Guadalajara on March 17.

Though it failed, the rebels won a smashing

victory at the Battle of Tepatitlan against

Saturnino Cedillo, led by General Pablo

Rodriguez, in the heart of Los Altos on April

19, 1929.

Unfortunately, Vega, who designed the plan

that won the victory, was killed in the

engagement.

Father Vega was a vigilante with multiple

vendettas and violent tendencies that are

unusual for a priest.

Allies

The "concentration" policy, rather than suppressing the revolt, gave it new life as thousands of men began to aid and join the rebels out of resentment for their treatment by the government.

When rain came, the peasants were allowed to return to the harvest, and there was now more support than ever for the Cristeros.

By August 1927, they had consolidated their movement and had begun constant attacks on federal troops garrisoned in their towns.

They would soon be joined by Enrique

Gorostieta, a retired general hired by the

National League for the Defense of Religious

Liberty.

On June 21, 1927, the first Women's Brigade

was formed in Zapopan.

It began with 16 women and one man, but after

a few days, it grew to 135 members and soon

came to number 17,000.

Its mission was to obtain money, weapons,

provisions, and information for the combatant

men and to care for the wounded.

By March 1928, some 10,000 women were involved in the struggle, with many smuggling weapons into combat zones by carrying them in carts filled with grain or cement.

By the end of the war, it had numbered some 25,000.

With close ties to the church and the clergy, the De La Torre family was instrumental in bringing the Cristero Movement to northern Mexico.

The family, originally from Zacatecas and Guanajuato, moved to Aguascalientes and then, in 1922, to San Luis Potosi. It moved again to

Tampico for economic reasons and finally to

Nogales to escape persecution from authorities

because of its involvement in the church and

the rebels.

Anacleto Gonzalez Flores

Anacleto Gonzalez Flores was a Mexican

Catholic and lawyer.

This was the second of twelve children born to

the poor family of Valentin Gonzalez Sanchez

and Maria Flores Navarro.

Anacleto Gonzalez Flores was baptized the day

after his birth.

A Roman Catholic priest who was a friend of

the family recognized Gonzales's intelligence

and recommended him for the minor seminary.

There, Gonzales excelled and earned the

nickname "Maestro."

After deciding that he did not have the calling to Holy Orders, Gonzalez began the study of law at the Escuela Libre de Derecho in Guadalajara and became an attorney in 1922. Gonzalez would eventually marry Maria Concepcion Guerrero, and they had two children.

Gonzalez would attend Mass daily and engage in numerous acts of charity, including visiting prisoners and teaching them the catechism. Gonzalez became an activist, led the Catholic Association of Mexican Youth (ACJM), and founded the magazine La Palabra, which

attacked the anticlerical and anti-Catholic

articles of the Constitution of 1917.

Gonzalez was the founder and president of the

Popular Union (UP), which organized Catholics

to resist the persecution of the church.

Originally, Gonzalez supported passive

resistance against the government since he had

studied the methods of Gandhi.

However, in 1926, he learned of the murder of

four members of the Catholic Association of

Mexican Youth and joined the National League

for the Defense of Religious Freedom as a result.

This motivated him to support the coming rebellion and organize resistance movements.

They described Mexico as a jail for the Catholic Church.

Gonzalez is not worried about defending the Catholic Church's material interests because these come and go, but he is more concerned with its spiritual interests.

Gonalzez promised he would defend these interests because he believed that they were necessary to obtain salvation.

In January 1927, after they had endured religious persecution and state atheism, Mexican Catholics took up arms and set off the Cristero War.

Gonzalez did not take up arms but gave speeches that encouraged Catholics to support the Cristeros with money, food, accommodation, and clothing.

He wrote pamphlets and gave speeches that supported his opposition to the anticlerical government.

Seeking to crush the rebellion, the Mexican government sought to capture the leaders of the Popular Union and the National League for the Defense of Religious Freedom.

Gonzalez was captured and framed with charges that he murdered an American, Edgar Wilkens, but the government knew that Wilkens had been killed by a robber named Guadalupe Zuno.

During his martyrdom, Gonzalez was tortured,

which included being hung by his thumbs,

which resulted in them being pulled out of their

sockets, having his shoulder fractured with a

rifle butt, and having the bottom of his feet

slashed.

On April 1, 1927, Gonzalez was executed by

firing squad.

Gonzalez's last words were "Hear Americas for

the second time: I die, but God does not! Viva

Cristo Rey!"

Edgar Wilkens's widow, who knew that

Gonzalez had been framed, wrote a letter of

protest to Washington, D.C., which exonerated

Gonzalez.

A letter requesting Gonzalez's execution

arrived shortly after he had been shot to death

by firing squad.

Gonzalez was like a Mexican Gandhi or Martin

Luther King Jr. who believed in equality and

fairness regardless of religion or personal

beliefs.

Gonzalez was a master orator who encouraged

others to do the right thing and stand up for

what was right.

Jose Sanchez del Rio

Jose Sanchez del Rio was a Catholic altar boy and martyr during the Cristero War.

The Cristero War began when the government began eliminating church privileges and seizing church properties throughout the country, in accordance with anti-clerical laws written into the Mexican Constitution.

President Plutarco Elias Calles, who took office in 1924, focused on the Roman Catholic Church, which led to the seizure of church property, the closing of religious schools and convents, and the exile or execution of priests.

Jose Sanchez del Rio was born on March 28, 1913, in Sahuayo, Michoacan.

Jose attended school first in his hometown, then in Guadalajara, in Jalisco.

When the Cristero War broke out in 1926, his brothers joined the rebel forces, but his mother would not allow him to take part.

His desire to join the Cristeros started when his priest was killed by a firing squad in front of the church as Jose hid in the church's bell tower.

The rebel general, Prudencio Mendoza Alcazar, also refused his enlistment.

Jose insisted that he wanted the chance to give his life for Jesus Christ and go to heaven. Mendoza relented and allowed Jose to become the flagbearer of the Cristero War.

The Cristeros nicknamed him Tarcisius, after the early Christian saint who was martyred for protecting the Eucharist from desecration. During heavy fighting on January 25, 1928, a Cristero soldier's horse was killed, and Jose gave his horse to the man so that he could flee.

Jose then sought cover and fired at the enemy until they ran out of ammunition.

The government troops captured Jose and imprisoned him.

It was later reported that Jose was captured by government forces, who ordered him to renounce his faith in Christ under the threat of death.

Jose refused to accept apostasy and was to be executed for his faith.

To break his resolve, he was made to watch the hanging of another Cristero that they had in custody, but instead Jose encouraged the man, saying that they would soon meet again in heaven after death.

In prison, Jose prayed the Rosary daily and wrote an emotional letter to his mother, saying that he was ready to fulfill the will of God, to whom he dedicated himself.

Jose's father attempted to raise a ransom to save him but was not able to appease the government in time to do so, thus failing to secure the release of his son.

Gruesome events transpired after the government's failure to break Jose's resolve on the evening of February 10, 1928.

Mexican government forces cut the bottom of Jose's feet and obliged him to walk around the town toward the cemetery.

They also cut him multiple times with a machete until he was bleeding from several wounds.

Jose cried and moaned with pain, but he did not give in or renounce his faith.

At times, they stopped him and said, 'If you shout, "Death to Christ the King," we will spare your life'.

Jose would only shout, 'I will never give in. Viva Cristo Rey!'"

Jose was then led to his grave while being forced to walk on salt as the soles of his feet were skinned.

Jose's parents met him at his grave and told them they would see them in heaven soon, before he was impaled by a machete and thrown into the grave to die from loss of blood.

He was 14 years old when he died on February 10, 1928.

The death of this child for his faith reignited the Cristeros, who rallied around the martyrdom of a child who was murdered for his faith by the Mexican government, ultimately leading to the last standstill Battle of Jalisco in 1929 that ended the Cristero War.

Aftermath

The government often did not abide by the terms of the 1929 truce.

For example, it executed some 500 Cristero leaders and 5,000 other Cristeros.

Particularly offensive to Catholics after the supposed truce was Calles's insistence on a complete state monopoly on education, which suppressed all Catholic education and introduced secular education in its place.

Calles's military persecution of Catholics would be officially condemned by Mexican President

Lazaro Cardenas and the Mexican Congress in

1935.

Between 1935 and 1936, Cardenas had Calles

and many of his close associates arrested and

forced them into exile soon afterwards as

punishment for the Cristero War.

Freedom of worship was no longer suppressed,

but some states still refused to repeal Calles's

policy.

Relations with the church improved under

President Cardenas.

The government's disregard for the Church, however, did not relent until 1940, when President Manuel Avila Camacho, a practicing Catholic, took office.

Church buildings in the country still belonged to the Mexican government during this time, and the nation's policies regarding the church still fell under federal jurisdiction.

Under Camacho, the bans against Church anticlerical laws were no longer enforced anywhere in Mexico.

Between 1926 and 1934, at least 40 priests were killed. There were 4,500 priests serving the people before the rebellion, but by 1934, there were only 334 licensed by the government to serve 15 million people.

The rest had been eliminated by emigration, expulsion, and assassination.

By 1935, 17 states had no priests at all.

The end of the Cristero War affected emigration to the United States.

The Cristeros made up 5 percent of Mexico's population, and many of them fled to America to escape persecution.

Many of them also made their way to Los Angeles, where they found a protector in John Joseph Cantwell, the bishop of what was then the Los Angeles-San Diego diocese.

Under Archbishop Cantwell's sponsorship, the Cristero refugees became a substantial community in Los Angeles, California.

In 1934, there was a parade of 40,000 Cristeros through Los Angeles.

The Calles Law was repealed after Cardenas became president in 1934.

Cardenas earned respect from Pope Pius XI and befriended Mexican Archbishop Luis Maria Martinez, a major figure in Mexico's Catholic Church who successfully persuaded Mexicans to obey the government's laws peacefully.

The Church refused to back Mexican insurgent Saturnino Cedillo's failed revolt against Cardenas, although Cedillo endorsed more power for the Church.

Cardenas's government continued to suppress religion in the field of education during his administration.

The Mexican Congress eventually amended Article 3 of the Constitution in October 1934, and the amendment was later ignored by President Manuel Avila Camacho who officially repealed it from the Constitution in 1946.

Constitutional bans against the Church would not be enforced anywhere in Mexico during Camacho's presidency.

The promotion of socialist education met with strong opposition in some parts of academia and in areas that had been controlled by the Cristeros.

Pope Pius XI also published the encyclical Firmissimam constantiam on March 28, 1937, expressing his opposition to the "impious and corruptive school" and his support for Catholic action in Mexico.

Many of those who had been associated with the Cristeros took up arms again as independent rebels and were followed by some other

Catholics, but unarmed public school teachers were now among the main targets of independent atrocities associated with the rebels.

Conclusion

The Cristero War was very significant to current events.

It caused the deaths of many Catholics in Mexico due to persecution, intolerance, and fascism.

It's obvious that the Cristero War had an impact on present-day Mexico, considering the fact that there is smuggling and illegal immigration along the U.S.-Mexico border and the fact that 8 out of 10 Mexicans are now Catholic.

Bibliography

Benedict XVI (2005). "Apostolic Letter by which The Supreme Pontiff Benedict XVI has Raised to The Glory of The Altars". Libreria Editrice Vaticana.

Booth, George C. "Mexico's school-made society." Stanford University Press. 1941.

Catholic News Agency. "14 year-old Mexican martyr to be beatified Sunday". Catholic News Agency. Retrieved March 19, 2016.

Check, Christopher. "Catholic Answers Magazine." *¡Viva Cristo Rey!* Web. 08

Mar. 2016. <http://www.catholic.com/
magazine/artices/¡viva-cristo-rey>.

Check, Christopher. "The Cristeros and the
Mexican Martyrs". *This Rock*. September
2007.

"De La Torres Family Papers". University of
Arizona. http://www.azarchivesonline.org/
xtf/view?docId=ead/uoa/UAMS420.xml&
doc.view=content&brand=default&anchor.
id=0

de Segovia, Antonio (1989). Great Witnesses to our Diocese. 1989 1 (1): 1. Retrieved September 13, 2022.

Gonzalez, Luis, (John Upton translator), "San Jose de Gracia: Mexican Village in Transition". University of Texas Press, 1982.

Grabman, Richard. "Gorostieta and the Cristiada: Mexico's Catholic Insurgency of 1926-1929".eBook, Editorial Mazatlan, 2012.

Greene, Graham. The Lawless Roads, Prologue (Penguin Classics 1993)

Guizar, Jesus Degollado. *Memoirs of Jesus Degollado Guizar, Last General In Chief of the Cristero Army*. Editorial Jus, 1957.

Hernandez Hurtado, Juan Francisco (2003). Judle from Tepa. Land of Christians. History of Victoriano Ramirez and the crissy revolution in the highlands of Jalisco. Center for Mexican and Central American Studies. ISBN 9782821846104.

Hurtado, Hernandez and Francisco, Juan.
"Capitulo XXVI. Muerte de Victoriano en
el Pcio de Tepa", (2014).

Jimenez Campo, Laura (2005). D.R. editorial,
ed. The New Baetos Cristeros. D.R.
Editorial.

Jowett, Philip. "Liberty or Death: Latin
American Conflicts, 1900–70.
Bloomsbury Publishing. 2019.

Krauze, Enrique. "Mexico: biography of power:
a history of modern Mexico, 1810–1996.
HarperCollins. 1998.

Levillain, Philippe. "The Papacy: An

Encyclopedia". Routledge. 2002.

Lichon, Katy et al. "¡Viva Cristo Rey!

Honoring Saint Jose Sanchez del Rio",

University of Notre Dame

Lopez-Menendez, Marisol (2016). Miguel Pro:

Martyrdom, Politics, and Society in

Twentieth-Century Mexico. Lexington

Books. ISBN 978-1-4985-0426-3.

Meyer, Jean A. (1994). Apogee of the Cristero

Movement. The Christian: The War of the

Christians (22 edition). 21st Century.

ISBN 97896823198159789682319815.

Meyer, Jean A. (2005). The war. The Christian:

The War of the Christians 3 (22 edition).

21st Century. pp. 106,266. ISBN

97896823198159789682319815.

Meyer, Jean. "La Cristiada: A Mexican People's

War on Religious Liberty". SquareOne

Publishers.

Meyer, Jean. The Cristero Rebellion: The

Mexican People between Church and

State, 1926–1929. Cambridge: Cambridge University Press. 1976.

Parsons, Wilfrid. Mexican Martyrdom.2003 Kessinger Publishing, ISBN 0-7661-7246-5

Religion en Libertad. "At 14, the martyr Jose Sanchez had more value than all the enemy troops: model for the young". Religion en Libertad. March 19, 2016.

Rieff, David; "Nuevo Catholics"; *The New York Times* Magazine; December 24, 2006.

Sherman, John W. The Mexican right: the end
of revolutionary reform, 1929–1940.
Greenwood Publishing Group. 1997,

Toro, Ross. "The World's Catholic Population
(Infographic)." *LiveScience*. TechMedia
Network, 19 Feb. 2013. Web. 19 Mar.
2016. <http://www.livescience.com
/27244-the-world-s-catholic-population-
infographic.html>.

Tuck, Jim, The Anti-clerical Who Led a
Catholic Rebellion, Latin American
Studies

Tuck, Jim, The Holy War in Los Altos: A
Regional Analysis of Mexico's Cristero
Rebellion, University of Arizona Press,
1982

Van Hove, Brian "Blood-Drenched Altars"
Faith & Reason. 1994.
http://www.ewtn.com/
library/HOMELIBR/FR94204.TXT

Vatican News Services. Jose Anacleto
Gonzalez Flores and eight Companions.
Vatican News Services. November 20,
2005

Vazquez, Carlos Perez (Translator). "The

Political Constitution of the Mexican

United States". Universidad Nacional

Autonoma de Mexico. 2005.

www.juridicas.unam.mx/infjur/leg/const

mex/pdf/consting.pdf

Young, Julia G. "Smuggling for Christ the

King: The Cristero War | OUPBlog."

Smuggling for Christ the King. 23 July

2015. Web. 08 Mar. 2016.

<http://blog.oup.com/2015/07/mexican-

catholics-cristero-war/>.